Little **BIG** Chats

My Early Warning Signs

by Jayneen Sanders

illustrated by Cherie Zamazing

My Early Warning Signs
Educate2Empower Publishing an imprint of
UpLoad Publishing Pty Ltd
Victoria Australia
www.upload.com.au

First published in 2021

Written by Jayneen Sanders
Illustrations by Cherie Zamazing

Jayneen Sanders asserts her right to be identified as the author of this work.
Cherie Zamazing asserts her right to be identified as the illustrator of this work.

Designed by Stephanie Spartels, Studio Spartels

ISBN: 9781761160264 (hbk) 9781761160127 (pbk)

NATIONAL
LIBRARY
OF AUSTRALIA

A catalogue record for this
book is available from the
National Library of Australia

Disclaimer: The information in this book is advice only, written by the author based on
her advocacy in this area, and her experience working with children as a classroom teacher
and mother. The information is not meant to be a substitute for professional advice. If you
are concerned about a child's behavior seek professional help.

Using Little BIG Chats

The *Little BIG Chats* series has been written to assist parents, caregivers and educators to have open and age-appropriate conversations with young children around crucial, and yet at times, 'tough' topics. And what better way than using children's picture books! Some pages will have questions for your child to interact with and discuss. Feel free to use these questions and the Discussion Questions provided on page 19 of this book to help you assist your child with the topic being explored. Stop at any time to unpack the text together; and try to follow your child's lead wherever that conversation may take you! So, please, get comfy and start some empowering 'chats' around some BIG topics with your child.

The Body Safety titles should ideally be read in the following order:
Consent, *My Safety Network*, *My Early Warning Signs*,
Private Parts are Private, and *Secrets and Surprises*.
The remaining titles can be read in any order.

Meet the Little BIG Chats KIDS

Theodore

Asha

Ardie

Tom

Jun

Jamie

Belle

Lisa

Maisy

Tilly

Maya

Ben

Hi! I'm Tilly.
Today we're
learning about our
Early Warning Signs.

Did you know that
your body is very smart?
If you feel unsafe it will
let you know.

WHEN DO YOU
FEEL SAFE?

WHEN DO YOU
FEEL UNSAFE?

You might get a
sick tummy or your
legs might shake.

These feelings in
your body are called
your Early Warning Signs.

There are many kinds
of Early Warning Signs.

You might feel only one
or two, or you might
feel many of your
Early Warning Signs.

Look at this boy.

He has lots of
Early Warning Signs.

Shaky all over

Hair feels like it is standing on end

Sweaty brow

Starts to cry

Heart beats fast

Goosebumps

Feels sick in the tummy

Sweaty palms

Needs to go to the toilet

HAVE YOU EVER FELT ANY OF THESE EARLY WARNING SIGNS?

Wobbly legs

If you ever feel any of your
Early Warning Signs,
you should tell a trusted
grown-up on your
Safety Network straightway.

They will listen to you
and they will help you.

WHO ARE THE GROWN-UPS ON YOUR SAFETY NETWORK?

13

Sometimes we might get
our Early Warning Signs just
because we are excited!

And that's okay!

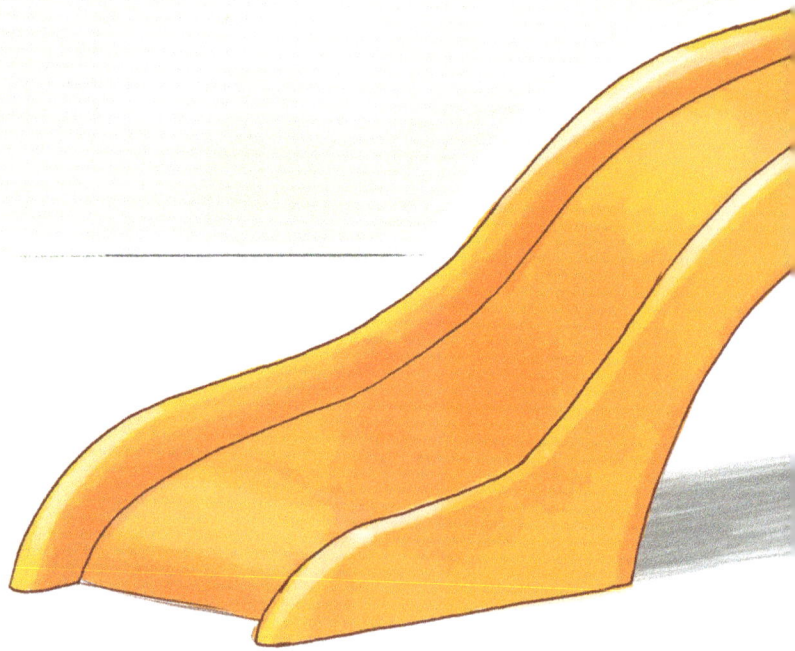

WHAT EXCITING
THINGS DO YOU
LIKE TO DO?

WHAT EARLY
WARNING SIGNS
MIGHT YOU GET?

But if you get your Early Warning Signs when you feel unsafe, scared or worried, you need to tell a trusted grown-up on your Safety Network straightway.

Your body is very smart!

It lets you know
when you feel unsafe.

My body is
very smart!

DISCUSSION QUESTIONS
for Parents, Caregivers and Educators

The following Discussion Questions are intended as a guide, and can be used to initiate open, age-appropriate and empowering conversations with your child.

This book explores children's Early Warning Signs and how they can act upon them immediately. Adults and children alike, all experience Early Warning Signs when they feel unsafe, worried, scared and/or excited. Helping children to understand our body's natural reaction to feeling unsafe and alerting them to know exactly what to do is empowering and crucial in keeping children safe.

Page 5
Introduce Tilly. Ask, 'What do you think our "Early Warning Signs" might be?'

Pages 6-7
Ask, 'How might your body let you know if you feel unsafe? Is Tilly feeling unsafe right now? Why do you say that?' Note: we would never want children to feel scared of dogs, so lead the discussion to Tilly getting a big fright when the dog started barking.

Pages 8-9
Ask, 'What does your body do if you feel unsafe, worried or scared?' Note: you could list your child's Early Warning Signs.

Pages 10-11
Talk about the little boy's Early Warning Signs with your child. Read and discuss each label. Ask, 'Can you think of any other Early Warning Signs a person might get?'

Pages 12-13
Ask, 'What should you do if you get any of your Early Warning Signs?' Praise your child's answer which should be, 'Tell a trusted grown-up on my Safety Network straightaway.' Note: encourage your child to decide on three to five adults that they trust and help them form a Safety Network. (See the book 'My Safety Network' included in the Little BIG Chats series.)

Pages 14-15
Ask, 'What Early Warning Signs might you get when you are excited? Do you ever feel a little bit excited and a little bit scared all at once? When have you ever felt that way? Is it okay to feel like that sometimes? When might it be okay? Can you give me some examples?' For example, on a fair ride, on a big waterslide, riding a pony, climbing a tree, etc.

Pages 16-17
Reinforce the text on this page. Ask, 'Why might Tilly feel unsafe near the teenagers? What are some of the Early Warning Signs she might get?' Refer back to page 11 for ideas and to reinforce the Early Warning Signs a child may experience.

Page 18
Ask, 'Why is your body very smart? How does it let you know when you feel unsafe?'

For more books that include Early Warning Signs concepts, see Jayneen Sanders' children's books 'No Means No!'; 'My Body! What I Say Goes!'; 'Let's Talk About Body Boundaries, Consent and Respect'; 'ABC of Body Safety and Consent' and 'Some Secrets Should Never Be Kept'.

Little BIG Chats

A series of 12 little books to help kids unpack BIG topics

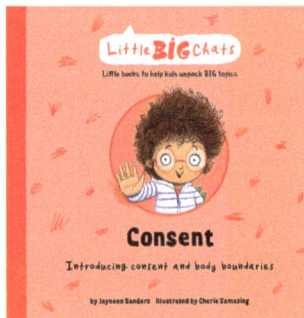

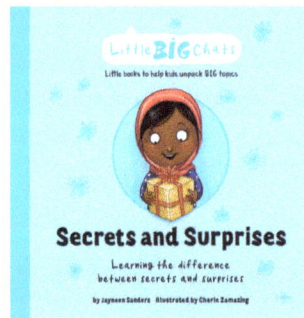

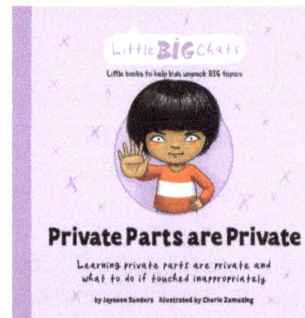

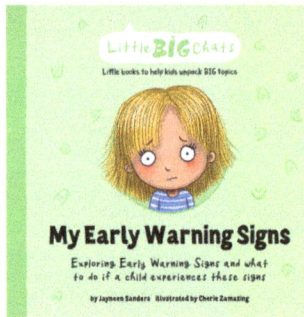

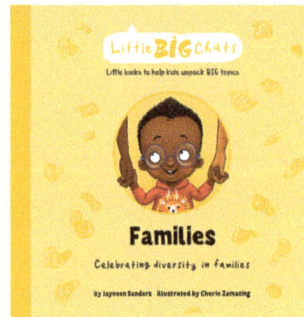

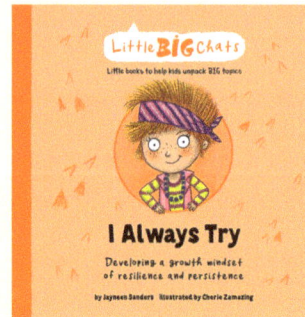

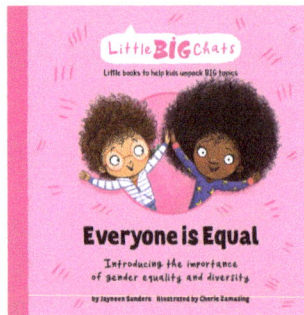

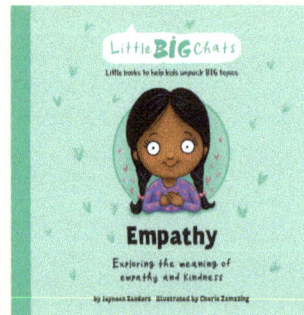

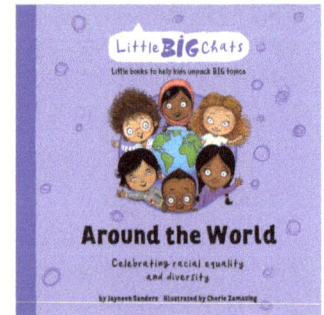

Little BIG Chats
Little books to help kids unpack BIG topics

Consent

Introducing consent and body boundaries

by Jayneen Sanders   Illustrated by Cherie Zamazing

Little BIG Chats
Little books to help kids unpack BIG topics

Secrets and Surprises

Learning the difference between secrets and surprises

by Jayneen Sanders   Illustrated by Cherie Zamazing

Little BIG Chats
Little books to help kids unpack BIG topics

Private Parts are Private

Learning private parts are private and what to do if touched inappropriately

by Jayneen Sanders   Illustrated by Cherie Zamazing

Little BIG Chats
Little books to help kids unpack BIG topics

My Safety Network

Introducing a Safety Network (3 to 5 trusted adults a child can go to if they feel unsafe)

by Jayneen Sanders   Illustrated by Cherie Zamazing

Little BIG Chats
Little books to help kids unpack BIG topics

My Early Warning Signs

Exploring Early Warning Signs and what to do if a child experiences these signs

by Jayneen Sanders   Illustrated by Cherie Zamazing

Little BIG Chats
Little books to help kids unpack BIG topics

Families

Celebrating diversity in families

by Jayneen Sanders   Illustrated by Cherie Zamazing

Little BIG Chats
Little books to help kids unpack BIG topics

I Always Try

Developing a growth mindset of resilience and persistence

by Jayneen Sanders   Illustrated by Cherie Zamazing

Little BIG Chats
Little books to help kids unpack BIG topics

Feelings

Understanding different feelings and emotions

by Jayneen Sanders   Illustrated by Cherie Zamazing

Little BIG Chats
Little books to help kids unpack BIG topics

Everyone is Equal

Introducing the importance of gender equality and diversity

by Jayneen Sanders   Illustrated by Cherie Zamazing

Little BIG Chats
Little books to help kids unpack BIG topics

Empathy

Exploring the meaning of empathy and kindness

by Jayneen Sanders   Illustrated by Cherie Zamazing

Little BIG Chats
Little books to help kids unpack BIG topics

Mindfulness

Exploring the importance of mindfulness and learning calming skills

by Jayneen Sanders   Illustrated by Cherie Zamazing

Little BIG Chats
Little books to help kids unpack BIG topics

Around the World

Celebrating racial equality and diversity

by Jayneen Sanders   Illustrated by Cherie Zamazing